PROMOTABILITY INDEX®

HOW PROMOTABLE ARE YOU?

Use this free career development tool at
http://bit.ly/PromotabilityIndex
to find out!

Being promotable exponentially enhances your career. It means you have highly sought-after skills valued in your current or future role. You're at the top of your game, and you have career choices.

I developed the **Promotability Index (PI)** to help you assess where you are in your corporate career and provide you with a self-development checklist to keep progressing. My goal is to equip you with an awareness of the qualities and behaviors possessed by corporate leaders and sought out by management teams, so that you know where to focus as you take charge of your success.

Take the Promotability Index and see where you stack up against the Five Key Elements. You'll receive a customized report based on your results.

Use this code for easy access to
the Promotability Index on all your digital devices.

PRAISE FOR *THE PI GUIDEBOOK* AND FOR WORKING WITH AMII BARNARD-BAHN

"I wish I had *The PI Guidebook* ten years ago. As someone who sits on the other side from people who want to be promoted, this is really helpful."

— Donna Lucas, CEO, Lucas Public Affairs

"*The PI Guidebook* provides practical steps to help leaders stand out in the areas that matter most."

— Dr. Tasha Eurich, New York Times best-selling author of *Insight* and *Bankable Leadership*

"An essential resource for those with aspirations to climb the corporate ladder in the most frictionless way."

— Feyzi Fatehi, CEO, Corent Technology

"The Promotability Index and *The PI Guidebook* together provide the ultimate toolkit for any professional to be a better leader, manager, and colleague. Amii challenges us, in her customarily inspirational and insightful way, to do and be our best."

— Marshall Goldsmith, *New York Times* best-selling author of *What Got You Here Won't Get You There,* and Thinkers 50 #1 Executive Coach

"I've used the PI within financial and university settings. My teams were able to leverage shared language about promotability within days. The PI measures behaviors that are often unspoken. *The PI Guidebook* provides clarity and a roadmap for employees wanting to make a greater impact. I recommend adding this to performance conversations, particularly for high performers."

— Erica Dias, Senior Vice President, Redwood Credit Union

"At long last, the Promotability Index has the perfect partner: *The PI Guidebook*. This quick read is loaded with vital 'how to' nuggets and fascinating background insights. If you'd like to clarify your potential pathways up any kind of career ladder, let this guidebook show you a better way. Amii Barnard-Bahn's extraordinarily helpful coaching perspective comes from a rare combination of high achievement in the C-suite, the courtroom, and the boardroom. You'll be hard pressed to find a better advisor."

— Dr. Paul L. Corona, Clinical Professor of Leadership, Kellogg School of Management at Northwestern University

"Amii's Promotability Index and *The PI Guidebook* offer a real opportunity to give women in the workplace, minority and otherwise, more control over their destiny, as they learn to step forward armed with the right tools, knowledge, and mindset to build the confidence they need to get what they deserve."

— Dr. Lilian Ajayi-Ore, Chief Learning Officer, Founder, and CEO, Global Connections for Women Foundation

"A practical guide applicable to anyone at every stage of their professional development. Amii Barnard-Bahn's success as a coach, mentor, and now author is deeply rooted in her rich experience and keen insights into what inspires us to reach our greatest potential while providing us with practical tools to do so. Don't miss this one!"

— Janet Kloenhamer, former President, Allianz of America Resolution Services, and Senior Vice President for Administration, General Counsel, and Corporate Secretary, Hawai'i Pacific University

"The most talented employees within our organizations are eager for upward mobility. They want opportunities to spread their wings and gain greater influence. When the path to those ambitions is obscure, unnavigable, or unavailable, our most talented people move on. Amii Barnard-Bahn's The Promotability Index and its accompanying handbook are a gold mine that will help ambitious and upwardly aspiring professionals to craft their custom roadmap, while helping those leaders responsible for stewarding talent to make sure there are pathways to help them realize their dream careers."

— Ron Carucci, Managing Partner, Navalent, and best-selling author of *Rising to Power* and *To Be Honest*

"Amii has compiled a practical and actionable set of essential tools that equip executives to assess and reflect on how they show up as leaders, and edit for growth and success. *The PI Guidebook* is a must-have for any leader's professional journey."

— Nicole Soluri, CEO, Professional BusinessWomen of California (PBWC)

"CEOs will say, 'Every business is a people business,' because they know that when businesses develop their people, productivity and profitability soar. Amii Barnard-Bahn's book is an organization's jet fuel and should be required reading for executives and managers. Amii's experience and uncanny insight have generated a transparent, easy to understand guide for developing an organization's most important asset—its people. Every CEO should mandate using the PI and *The PI Guidebook* for employee development."

— Mary Flipse, former Chief Legal and Administrative Officer, Tivity Health, Inc.

"Curating the world's largest community of professional coaches, we at WBECS come across many different tools and frameworks for coaches to use with their clients. *The PI Guidebook* offers some of the most practical for saving time, money, and mistakes and helping corporate leaders to do the right thing. What else could be more important?"

— Ben Croft, Founder and Chairman, WBECS Group, and Founder and Chairman, EthicalCoach

"Amii is a seasoned expert in human resources and human capital management. Her expertise is revealed in these pages. Amii has touched on every element of how to be promoted—in fact, how to control your own destiny. "

— Betsy Berkhemer-Credaire, CEO, 50/50 Women on Boards

"I resonate deeply with Amii's approach to promotability. Her guidebook and interactive assessment can help anyone clarify how to move forward faster in their career, by focusing on what matters most: relationships. She has created an invaluable toolset for leaders, coaches, and just about anyone involved in career and leadership development."

— Jeffrey Hull, PhD, author of *FLEX: The Art and Science of Leadership in a Changing World*, and Harvard Medical School psychologist

"Amii Barnard-Bahn does a masterful job in laying out a framework for achieving career success. *The PI Guidebook* outlines the criteria organizations use when determining who to invest in and promote. This book is a must read for anyone focused on developing their career."

— Janine Yancey, CEO, Emtrain

"No matter what stage you are in your career, you need a plan, a roadmap. Whether you are exploring in the early stages, establishing your career, or advancing to higher levels, *The PI Guidebook* will help you achieve your goals. It is simple, it is detailed, and it works! Enjoy the journey to creating a better and more fulfilling life at work and home."

— Chester Elton, best-selling author of *The Carrot Principle*, *Leading with Gratitude*, and *Anxiety at Work*

"Amii's Promotability Index is a straight-forward and actionable tool to guide career development conversations. As a former HR leader frequently coaching employees and developing coaching skills for HR business partners and talent professionals, I find the PI and *The PI Guidebook* incredibly useful."

— Paige Dickow, former Managing Director and HR leader, BlackRock

"Ever wonder why you're getting passed over for promotion on your way to the C-Suite? Amii Barnard-Bahn has created the Promotability Index and *The PI Guidebook* to level the playing field and give you the insider secrets on how to get ahead. This methodology is priceless!"

— Denise Brosseau, author of *Ready to Be a Thought Leader?*, and CEO, Thought Leadership Lab

THE PI GUIDEBOOK

*How the **Promotability Index®** Can Help You Get Ahead in Your Career*

Amii Barnard-Bahn

The PI Guidebook: How the Promotability Index® Can Help You Get Ahead in Your Career
Copyright © 2021 by Amii Barnard-Bahn. All rights reserved.
Published by Edgewater Press. *www.edgewaterpress.net*.

Aside from brief passages in a published review, no part of this book may be reproduced or transmitted in any form or by any means, electronic or mechanical, including all technologies known or later developed, without written permission from the publisher. For reprint permission write to *info.barnardbahn@gmail.com.*

Edgewater Press books are available at significant quantity discounts when purchased in bulk for sales promotions, client gifts, or corporate use. Special editions, including personalized covers, excerpts of existing books, or books with corporate logos, customized covers, and letters from the company or CEO printed in the front matter, can be created in large quantities for special needs. For details and discount information for both print and ebook formats, contact *info.barnardbahn@gmail.com.*

Promotability Index® is a registered trademark of Barnard-Bahn Coaching & Consulting.
All rights reserved.

Book design by Michelle Montbertrand

Paperback ISBN:	978-1-7370293-0-4
Hardcover ISBN:	978-1-7370293-3-5
Custom Interactive PDF ISBN:	978-1-7370293-1-1
Ebook ISBN:	978-1-7370293-2-8
Library of Congress Control #:	2021908026

To explore leadership coaching, speaking, and Promotability Index workshops for you or your organization, contact us at *barnardbahn.com.*

Printed in the United States

CONTENTS

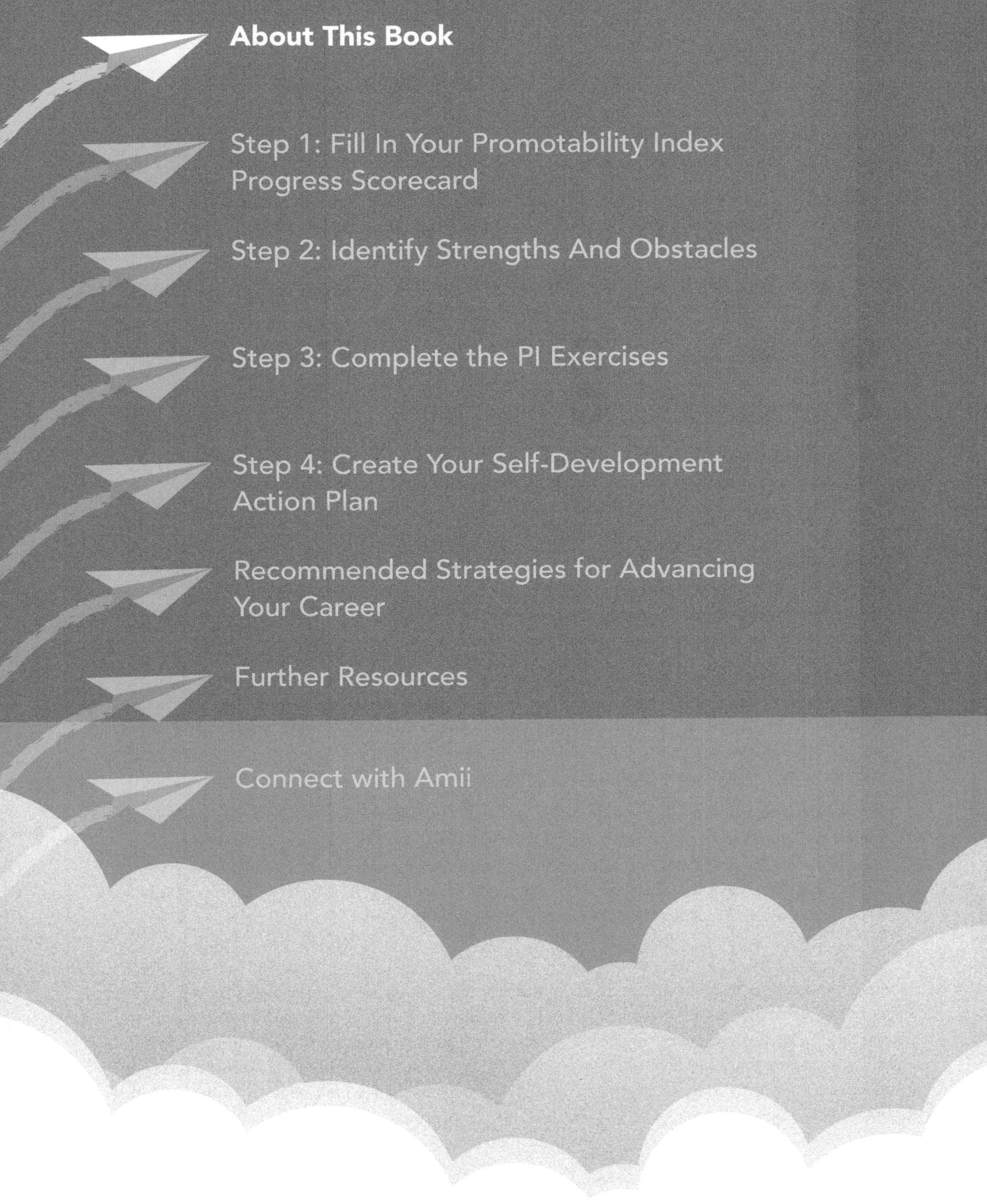

ABOUT THIS BOOK

Get ready for a transformative experience that will help you take clear and actionable steps to advance your career—wherever you are in your journey.

This book is a companion guide to the Promotability Index® (PI). You can download the PI at *barnardbahn.com/promotabilityindex*. Once you have completed the PI, use this book to get the most out of the results.

The PI assesses your abilities within five key elements used by management when deciding who to promote and invest in as leaders. These five elements are:

 Self-Awareness
 Strategic Thinking
 Thought Leadership
 External Awareness
 Executive Presence

The Promotability Index also gives you an overall gauge of where you are in your career development. Are you Exploring, Establishing, or Advancing? Understanding these three stages of your career's lifecycle can help you choose which areas to work on first to get you the results you are seeking.

The **Exploring** stage is early in your career, typically when you have finished your formal education and had a few different work experiences in varied roles or organizations. You are building technical proficiency in your chosen field or may still be exploring and seeking your niche, while building your professional network.

The **Establishing** stage comes after you have been working for several years with gradually increasing responsibility. You typically have direct reports and are learning to manage teams so they get results. You also likely have a strong network and sponsorship within your organization. Known for your area of expertise, you are working toward mastery and seeking cross-functional opportunities to expand strategic thinking, sponsorship, and your professional community.

The **Advancing** stage arrives when you have the passion and will to lead others, usually having first mastered and moved beyond your area of expertise. A systems thinker, you lead cross-functional teams and are sought out to provide strategic input on a variety of issues. You likely have the ability to exert influence, ask insightful questions, and facilitate the discussions and partnerships that lead to informed decisions.

While it's helpful to know which stage of career development you're in, it's also true that most careers do not follow a linear path. This book is designed to help you no matter where you are on that path. My hope is that using this guidebook will surface ideas and spark them into action. And if you consistently log and track your progress, you will keep yourself accountable to your goals. Have fun discovering what attracts you. It's exciting to unlock new skills and interests—and the self-knowledge you gain gives you power over your future.

©2021 Amii Barnard-Bahn

THE FIVE ELEMENTS OF PROMOTABILITY

Five crucial qualities, or elements, affect promotability.

Self-Awareness: A conscious knowledge and ongoing desire to understand and live in alignment with your personal values, feelings, motives, and interests.

External Awareness: The ability to accurately understand both the impact of your behavior on others and the impressions and perceptions others have of you. When you invest in external awareness, you gain valuable knowledge that enables you to build relationships with a wide variety of people, actively manage your reputation, and respond effectively in challenging situations.

Strategic Thinking: A cultivated and demonstrated ability to identify, analyze, and synthesize data from diverse sources to inspire fresh thinking, impact organizational outcomes, and create competitive advantage. For purposes of the PI, we are focused on the degree to which senior management views you as a strategic thinker.

Executive Presence: Inspiring confidence in others so they view you as a leader. It is comprised of three components that can be learned by anyone: presentation skills (excellent written and spoken communication, in-person and virtual), gravitas (well-prepared, calm, solution-oriented, confident, and in control at all times), and professional appearance (tailoring, clothing choices consistent with company culture, and good grooming).

Thought Leadership: Being respected, sought-after, and well-known as an expert in your chosen field because you help educate, improve, and add value to your industry as a whole.

I identified these five elements based on my experience working in corporations for over twenty years. Over the course of my corporate career I made my way up to several executive positions, including chief human resources officer, chief compliance officer, and chief administrative officer. I have overseen multiple functional areas within a company. I have built teams, hired and fired people, and led succession planning for multiple organizations. I saw who got promoted and why. I watched careers accelerate quickly and others fall behind (or implode). I led organizations through all financial cycles, from huge growth to reductions in force, and learned which skill sets are most valued and which are disregarded when the chips are down.

In this book I attempt to share everything I've learned (sometimes the hard way) about promotability. These lessons are a culmination of my corporate career, human resources experience, and executive coaching knowledge.

HOW TO USE THIS BOOK

Once you've reviewed your PI results (STEP 1), you'll identify strengths and obstacles (STEP 2) and choose exercises (STEP 3) that help you improve within the elements you want to focus on. You'll then create a self-development action plan (STEP 4), which will include regularly retaking the PI and evaluating your progress.

The PI is a resource you can revisit for the rest of your career to help you stay relevant and keep growing as you work toward the promotions you earn. This is the level of information I wish I had all along. Whether you're just starting your career, at mid-career, or entering your peak, the PI combined with this guidebook will help you each step of the way.

I've intentionally designed the PI and this guidebook to be flexible and customizable. You're in charge of your career, so you choose what works for you. Move toward what inspires you, and have fun on this journey to self-actualization. You don't need to complete every exercise in this book to progress—everyone has different working preferences (for example, some of us are extroverts and some of us are introverts), and some abilities will be more natural to you, while you may have to work harder to develop others. This book gives you a framework to understand the qualities and traits organizations consider when deciding who has potential and whom they're going to invest in.

To get the most out of this book, take the PI self-assessment, review your scores, pick one or two lower-scoring areas to improve, and then select from the corresponding exercises. Record them in the action plan, and set target dates and measures of success. (You might also wish to consult some of the additional resources listed at the end of the book.) If you adopt a habit of retaking the PI every twelve months or so and revising your plan accordingly, your PI score will improve, and so will your promotability.

APPLYING THE PROMOTABILITY INDEX TO YOUR CAREER

The Promotability Index is intended to be an integrated career and discovery tool for focusing on what you need based on your stage of professional development. With the help of this guidebook you can use the PI to identify areas to improve each time you revisit your career advancement plan.

Remember that every job is temporary. You rent your job; you don't own it. If you adopt this perspective and follow the principles in this guidebook, you will always be employable and never have to worry about overdependency on one job. Knowing your skills gives you choices that will empower you.

Keep in mind that while the PI will help you work toward earning a promotion, sometimes you will need to change jobs to keep learning and progressing. If your skills are strong, they will give you a leg up if you decide a move is in order.

As my mentor Marshall Goldsmith told me when I shared one of my past career disappointments, "Sometimes we are at the whim of the larger environment—and mistakenly think we have control." This book allows space for these revelations, so be sure to include self-reflection as you explore your options and make progress on your professional goals.

 ©2021 Amii Barnard-Bahn

If something scares you, that is a likely sign that you are avoiding that aspect. Get curious and think about why a particular action is challenging for you. Maybe you'll discover the big thing that is holding you back.

Success is a series of small steps taken consistently and with discipline. Don't take too much on at once, or you can easily get overwhelmed.

Read on to take the first step in setting goals based on your individual assessment results.

Everyone has their own path. This book offers you a number of options to choose from. Ultimately you know best what will work for you, and there is no one right way to progress through the book. Go toward what attracts you, and let your assessment results from the PI guide your focus.

WAYS TO USE THE PROMOTABILITY INDEX

The PI can complement and supplement the developmental part of your company's performance review process. Consider partnering with a mentor, mentee, or colleague for mutual support in following through with your action plans and to drive shared accountability for your continued success.

Individual Professionals
Use the PI to help you define goals and measure progress within your development plan.

Companies
Integrate the PI into your performance management process. Support your employees in advancing their career development by hosting a PI masterclass and Q&A, using the assessment and this book. Use the PI as a career development tool for employees in mentoring programs, employee resource groups, and diversity initiatives. Mid-sized to large companies should consider sponsoring a PI Coaching Circle, in which senior professionals can work with Amii to get the most out of the PI assessment and guidebook, enhanced by peer-to-peer sessions and one-to-one coaching with Amii.

Associations
Support your members in advancing their career development by hosting a live or virtual PI webinar and Q&A, using the PI assessment and this book.

Other Ways to Use the PI
Reach out and let me know how you or your organization has used the PI to help accelerate career progress.

ABOUT THE NOTES PAGES

Throughout the Guidebook you'll find blank pages with the heading "Notes." Use these pages to journal, plan, doodle, and dream about your career and your future success. Revisit them from time to time, and enjoy seeing where and how far you've gone.

NOTES

©2021 Amii Barnard-Bahn

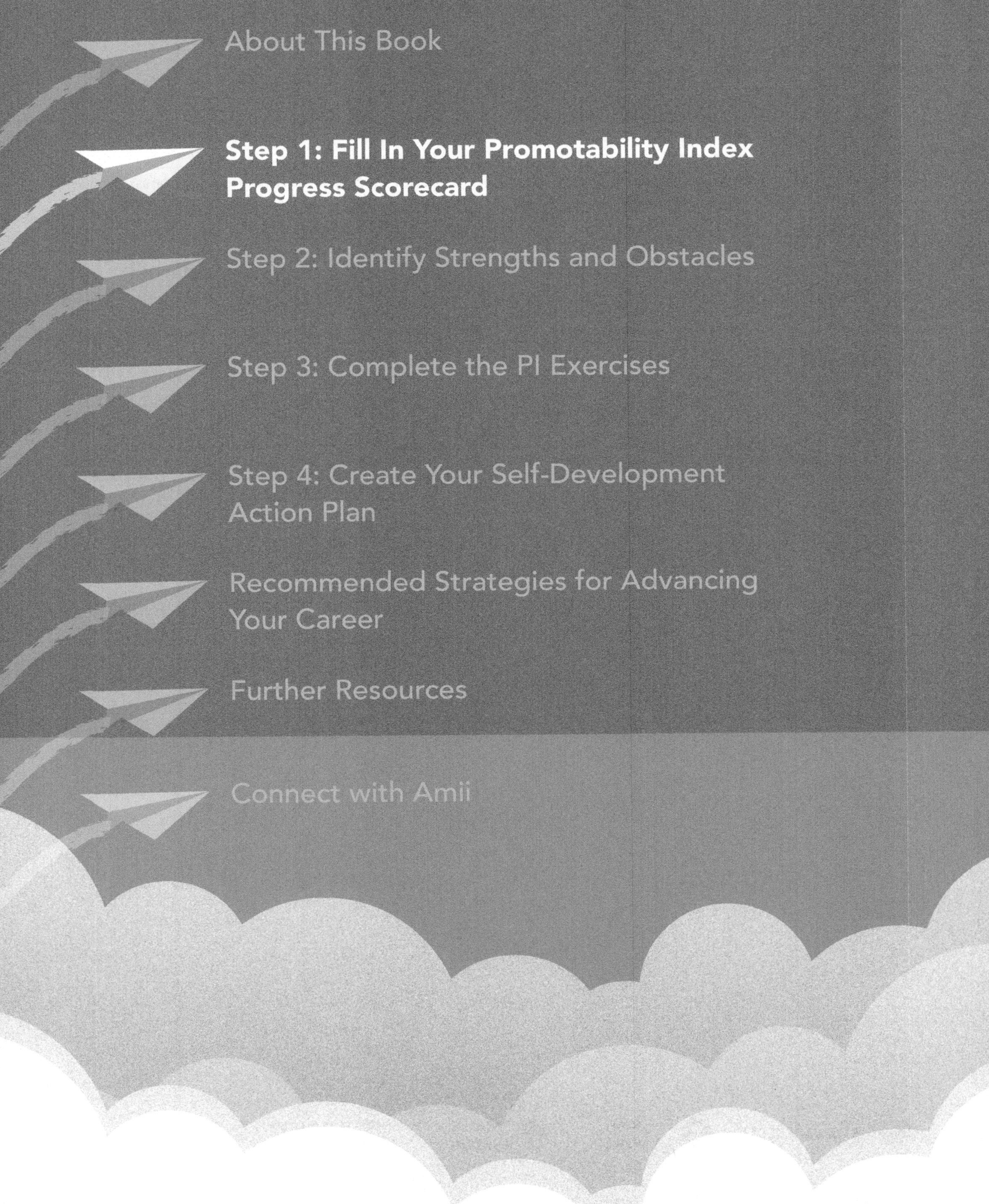
About This Book
Step 1: Fill In Your Promotability Index Progress Scorecard
Step 2: Identify Strengths and Obstacles
Step 3: Complete the PI Exercises
Step 4: Create Your Self-Development Action Plan
Recommended Strategies for Advancing Your Career
Further Resources
Connect with Amii

STEP 1

FILL IN YOUR PROMOTABILITY INDEX PROGRESS SCORECARD

Using your PI assessment, enter your scores in the chart below. I recommend retaking the assessment every twelve months or so to measure your progress. Be sure to pause and take time to celebrate your achievements.

Consider asking a mentor, colleague, or executive coach to be your accountability partner to support you in executing your plan based on your PI results.

Remember that big changes start with small steps. If you stay committed and take incremental action, you will keep advancing toward achieving your goals.

PI ASSESSMENT PROGRESS SCORECARD

DATE						TOTAL	NOTES

©2021 Amii Barnard-Bahn

ASSESSING YOUR PI SCORE: CAREER STAGES

Your PI score identifies which stage of career development you are in.

Up to 40 Points: EXPLORING. You're off to a great start! You have taken some key steps necessary to advance in your profession. Careers aren't built overnight; they are the result of a series of actions over time that lead to exceptional results. Be sure to review the five key elements, identify where you scored low, and pick two or three achievable actions to work on over the next six months. You'll want to periodically retake the PI and measure your progress. In this stage people often fail to get the feedback they need to improve. To progress in your career, it's critical to know yourself—your values, motivators, and work preferences—and eliminate any blind spots in how you view your performance compared to how others experience you. Proactively seek feedback and opportunities to increase your self-awareness and external awareness.

41 to 65 Points: ESTABLISHING. Fantastic! You have made solid strides in building your career, and you understand the importance of continued growth. You are well on your way to being promotable. Take a look at your lowest-scoring dimension, and invest in taking action in two or three areas that your organization values most.

66 to 82 Points: ADVANCING. Congratulations! You have built a solid career, are likely well-known both inside and outside of your company, and have good External Awareness as well as Self-Awareness and a proficient level of Executive Presence. You may be reaching peak promotability and are waiting for a promotion, or you are already at the top level of your organization's hierarchy for your role. At this level, it is critical to validate your self-assessment by getting unfiltered feedback from key stakeholders, such as through a 360 review. Once you have that feedback, use the PI as a guide to address those areas that can further polish your promotability and open up options beyond your core function into broader leadership roles (e.g. CEO, COO, CAO) as well as future corporate board appointments and advisory and consulting engagements.

NOTES

©2021 Amii Barnard-Bahn

STEP 2

IDENTIFY STRENGTHS AND OBSTACLES

Before digging into goal setting, you'll want to identify strengths that will support you in achieving your goals and the obstacles that may get in your way. The exercises below will help. Don't skip this step! You need a foundation for creating a bulletproof plan of action. Be sure to include these exercises in your action plan (STEP 4).

STRENGTHS

Consider all the various areas of support available to help get you to your goal.

What are your resources? For example: your education, business experience, professional certifications, publications, speaking engagements, awards. List them below.

What are your most relevant personal qualities? Think about your special gifts. If nothing immediately comes to mind, take a few minutes to think about the problems people most commonly come to you to help solve.

Who will support you in reaching your goals? For example: your family, friends, community, and professional network.

©2021 Amii Barnard-Bahn

OBSTACLES

Obstacles can be external or internal.

External Obstacles
These include structural constraints on your job, a lack of senior-level positions because your company is too small or your organization is in an unprofitable business cycle, or family or health factors that prevent you from relocating or traveling.

What are your external obstacles? For example: You work at a small company with limited opportunities for advancement. Or your family caretaking obligations prevent you from relocating.

....

....

....

Internal Obstacles
These include your thoughts, your mental model, and your personal habits that get in the way. For example: You're afraid to try something new. You're uncomfortable competing with colleagues. You worry about balancing your family responsibilities with increased career advancement.

What are your internal obstacles?

....

....

....

In the plan you create in Step 4, you will identify actions you can take to leverage your strengths and manage your obstacles.

NOTES

©2021 Amii Barnard-Bahn

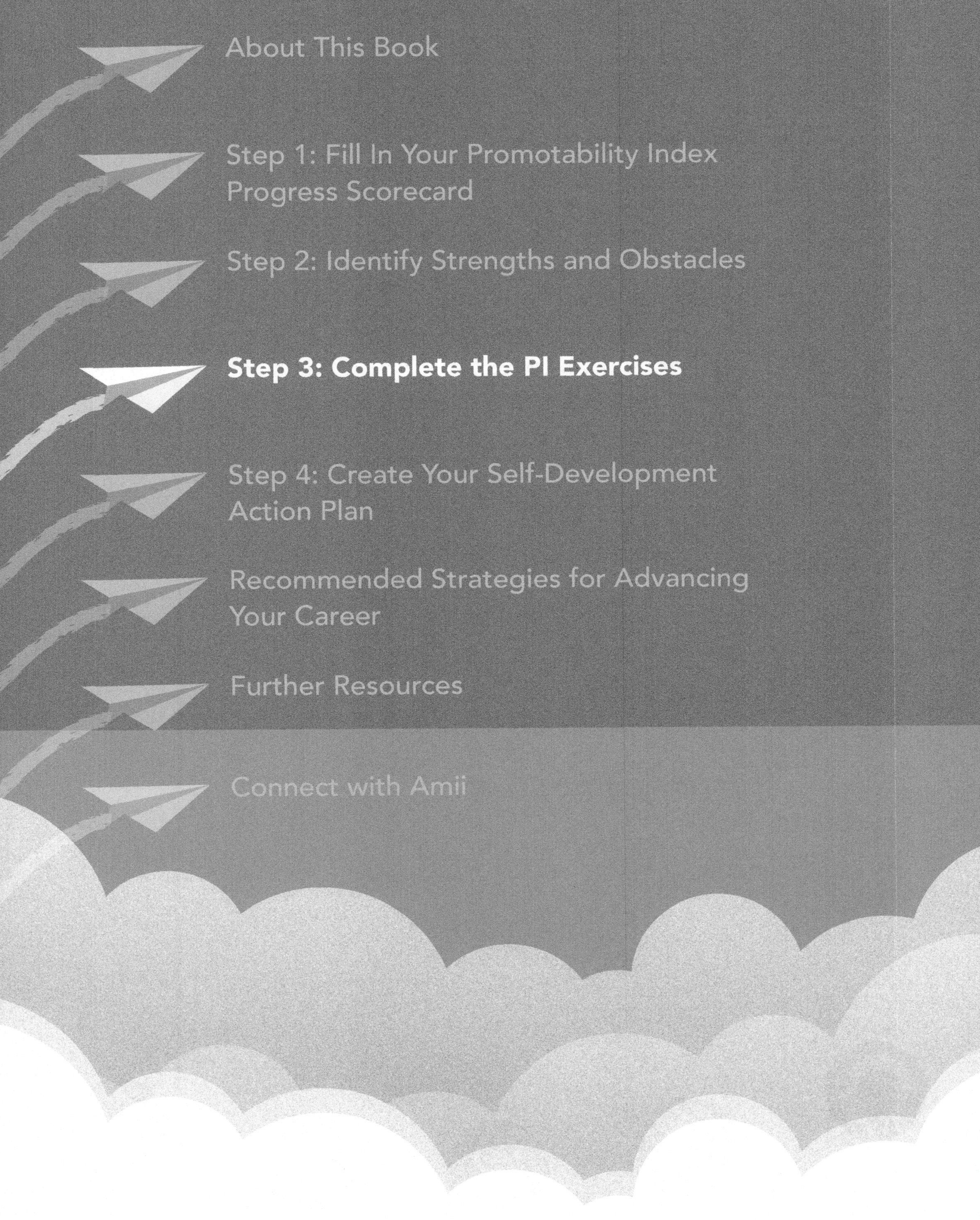
About This Book
Step 1: Fill In Your Promotability Index Progress Scorecard
Step 2: Identify Strengths and Obstacles
Step 3: Complete the PI Exercises
Step 4: Create Your Self-Development Action Plan
Recommended Strategies for Advancing Your Career
Further Resources
Connect with Amii

PROMOTABILITY INDEX

The Five Key Elements

STEP 3

COMPLETE THE PI EXERCISES

The following exercises are organized within each of the five key elements:

- Self-Awareness
- External Awareness
- Executive Presence
- Strategic Thinking
- Thought Leadership

Use your PI score to help you choose which elements you want to focus on, and enter at least two to three exercises for each element into your self-development plan on *page 62*.

PROMOTABILITY INDEX ELEMENT

Self-Awareness

SELF-AWARENESS

We are all broken. That's how the light gets in.

— Leonard Cohen, singer/songwriter

Self-awareness is the ability to be introspective, to accurately reflect on our behaviors, emotions, and attitudes. It is the foundational element of emotional intelligence, as defined by psychologist Daniel Goleman, and it has been cited as one of the top two reasons leaders succeed or fail.

Self-awareness enables you to view yourself objectively, without judgment. You need to know yourself well—your many gifts as well as behaviors and personality traits that can derail your career. An accurate and honest view of yourself enables you to make good decisions and quickly course-correct, if necessary.

Research from organizational psychologist and self-awareness researcher Dr. Tasha Eurich found that 95 percent of people think they are self-aware, but the real number is between 10 and 15 percent. So even if you scored high in this area, you should consider that your level of self-awareness may be much lower.

EXERCISES

Exercise #1: *Describing Your Personal Brand*

Reach out to three people who know you well in a work context. Ask them what three words come to mind when they think of you and your work. Write down their responses, and then reflect on them by answering the questions below.

Words others use to describe you:

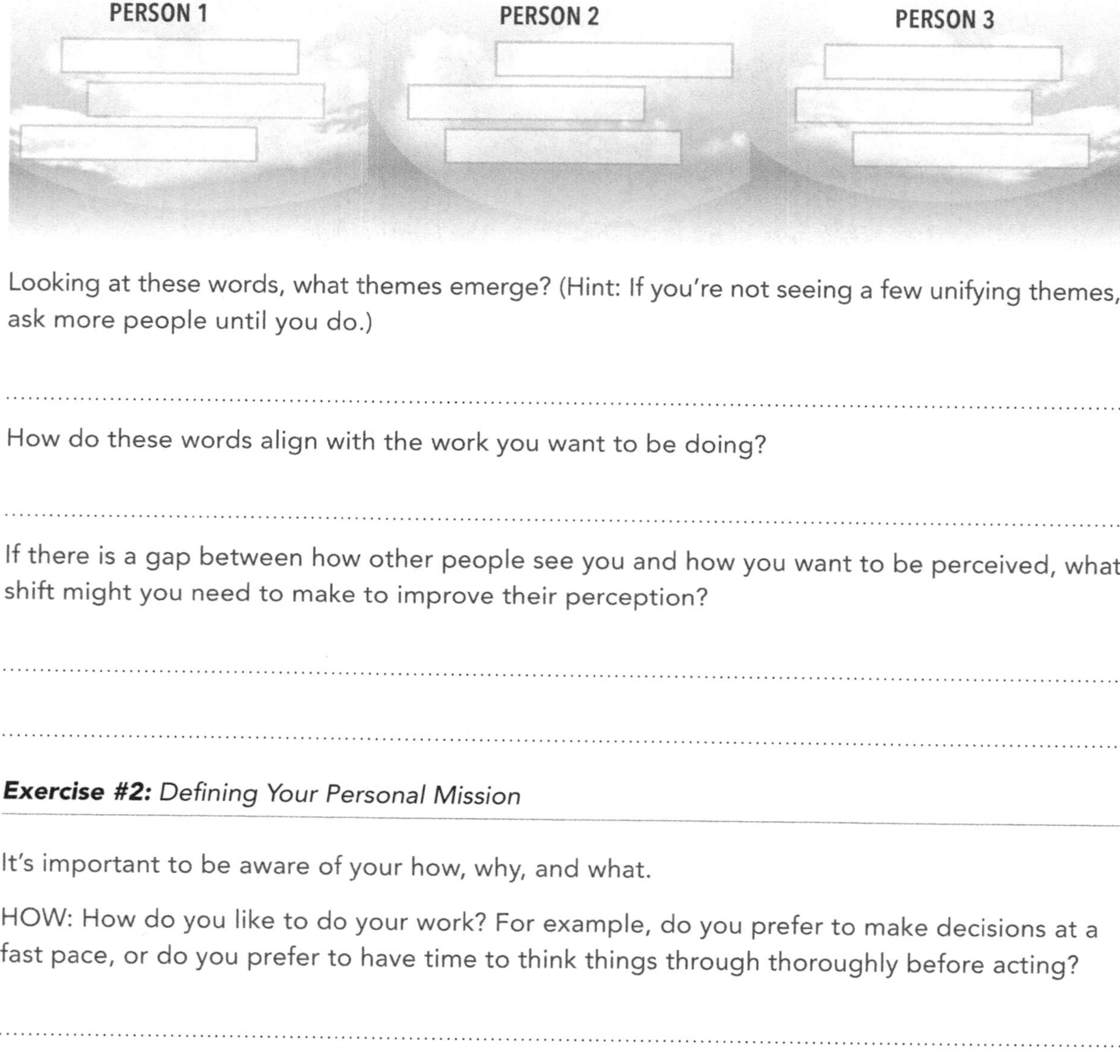

Looking at these words, what themes emerge? (Hint: If you're not seeing a few unifying themes, ask more people until you do.)

....

How do these words align with the work you want to be doing?

....

If there is a gap between how other people see you and how you want to be perceived, what shift might you need to make to improve their perception?

....

....

Exercise #2: *Defining Your Personal Mission*

It's important to be aware of your how, why, and what.

HOW: How do you like to do your work? For example, do you prefer to make decisions at a fast pace, or do you prefer to have time to think things through thoroughly before acting?

....

©2021 Amii Barnard-Bahn

WHY: Why do you do the work you do?

WHAT: What are you meant to do in this life?

Exercise #3: *Framing Your Questions*

Watch the TEDx Talk *Increase Your Self-Awareness with One Simple Fix* by Dr. Tasha Eurich (ted.com/talks/tasha_eurich_increase_your_self_awareness_with_one_simple_fix). Then answer the following questions.

What is the simple fix Dr. Eurich shares from her self-awareness research study?

Think of a challenge you are facing. How can you use Dr. Eurich's fix to reframe your challenge?

INSIGHT

All leaders are flawed. What distinguishes exceptional leaders is that they don't shy away from an awareness of their flaws. They identify their potential derailer behaviors and do the work to eliminate them. They ultimately accept themselves without judgment and then get to work on mitigating strategies for when problems arise.

Working with a coach is one of the best ways to improve self-awareness. Performance feedback, 360 reviews, and other input can help you become aware of how your leadership is perceived.

Exercise #4: *Owning Your Challenges*

What types of people do you find the most challenging? (For example: people who are shy, are blunt, only focus on work, or are overly accommodating.)

Why do you think these traits challenge you?

Think of a person you frequently work with who has these traits. How do you usually respond to them?

What is a different response you could choose?

What is another alternative response you could choose?

The next time you have an interaction with this person, choose an alternative response. Reflect on your experience here.

Exercise #5: *Getting the Full ROI from Mistakes*

What is one decision you have made in the past that you wish you could do over?

©2021 Amii Barnard-Bahn

What did you learn?

....

....

How does what you learned inform the choices you make today?

....

....

Exercise #6: *Getting Out of Your Own Way*

How do you get in your own way?

Describe this behavior in detail, starting with: I get in my own way when I

....

....

Describe the situations that trigger this behavior:

....

....

What different choice could you make next time?

....

....

INSIGHT

Our behaviors can feel automatic or out of our control at times. But if you cultivate an awareness of your typical response, you can intercept it and make a different choice in the moment and even going forward. It takes practice, but you can successfully change these behaviors.

NOTES

©2021 Amii Barnard-Bahn

NOTES

PROMOTABILITY INDEX ELEMENT

External Awareness

EXTERNAL AWARENESS

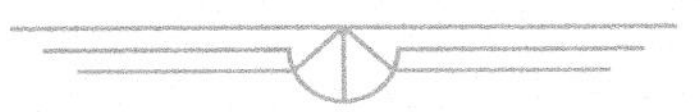

Fight for the things you care about, but do it in a way that will lead others to join you.

— Supreme Court Justice Ruth Bader Ginsburg

External awareness is how others experience you and your behavior—popularly expressed as your "personal brand." Even if you are doing and saying the right things, how and when you do so can be perceived in different ways—and perception matters.

Promotions aren't just about your skills; they're about your relationships. No matter where you are in your career, you need to have allies and sponsors to move forward. Someone needs to make that bet on you. Getting along well with others and knowing yourself are the top two factors affecting your success.

Look for opportunities to get feedback regularly from key stakeholders and trusted colleagues. Find out how others perceive you. This will help you become aware of behaviors that may be blocking or derailing your advancement.

EXERCISES

Exercise #7: *Fostering a Strong Relationship with Your Boss*

What is your boss's biggest pet peeve? (If you don't know, ask. In my experience, this often brings a smile, and they appreciate being asked.)

....

....

How does your boss like to be kept informed about your work? What medium do they prefer—text, IM, phone, email—and how often do they want to hear from you?

....

How would your boss rate you in terms of effective communication? Do you reach out at the right time, with the right amount of information? If you don't know, ask your boss to rate you on a scale of 1 to 5, with 5 being exceptionally effective.

....

Ask your boss to name one thing you could do to communicate more effectively. Write their answer here:

....

Keep in mind that if you want to get promoted, the right way to do anything on the job is the way your boss wants it done.

©2021 Amii Barnard-Bahn

Exercise #8: *Strengthening Stakeholder Relationships*

Identify five people who have the power to help you with your career.

What is their main goal for the coming year? If you don't know, ask.

What is one thing you can offer to help them achieve their goal?

Fill in the chart with their names and responses to the questions above.

NAME	GOAL	HOW I CAN HELP

INSIGHT

Reciprocity is powerful. Think about how you can nurture and build your network before you need it.

Exercise #9: *Eliminating Low-Value Work*

Think about one thing you could do to help your team with their workload. How can you make things more efficient and take useless work off their plate?

Solicit input at your next team meeting. Experiment with the most promising ideas.

INSIGHT

Meaningfully connecting with your team's day-to-day work will give you an opportunity to do things better. And asking how you can help will be appreciated, increasing employee loyalty and engagement.

Exercise #10: *Mentoring Others*

Think of a key leader who helped advise you along your career path.

What qualities do you admire most about them? How did they help you?

....

....

....

Next, identify one colleague outside your business unit whom you can commit to spending some time with each quarter. Make sure it's someone who welcomes your guidance. Commit to spending an hour with them once a month on a work issue they bring to you.

Name of potential mentee: ....

I am committed to: ....

Notes and action plan:

....

....

....

INSIGHT

Be one of those people you admire. We learn best when we are teaching others. You'll also benefit from paying it forward. I love receiving notes from former team members and colleagues about what they're doing now and how our work together helped them. It's one of the reasons I became an executive coach.

©2021 Amii Barnard-Bahn

Exercise #11: *Saying No*

To a significant degree, being a great leader is directly tied to your ability to say no to the right things. Do you delegate an assignment, but then have trouble letting go, otherwise known as micromanaging? Do you address poor performance promptly after a pattern begins to emerge?

Think about a time when you had trouble saying no, even though you knew you should.

Describe the circumstances:

....

....

What makes it hard to say no? ....

....

What do you gain by saying yes? ....

....

What do you lose by saying yes? ....

....

What boundary will you set next time? ....

....

How will you hold yourself accountable to this commitment? ....

....

....

Exercise #12: *Taking Care of Your Health*

Rate how well you are taking care of your physical and mental health. Consider sleep (seven to eight hours are recommended for most adults), exercise, nutrition (drink more water!), personal time versus work time, and other physical and mental health goals—like laughing more.

For each area on the wheel, give yourself a rating between 1 (poor) and 10 (fabulous).

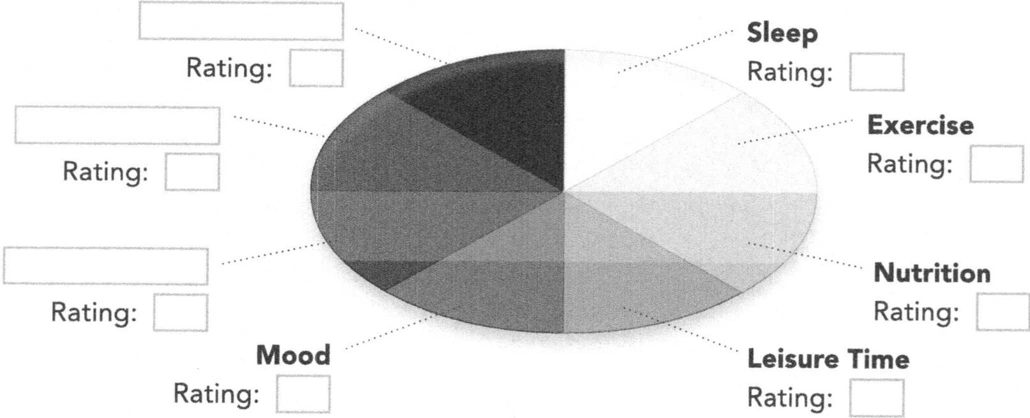

What is one thing you are motivated to start doing now to take better care of yourself? For example: take a twenty-minute walking break three times per week; drink one more glass of water each morning; or have one deep belly laugh every day.

....

....

INSIGHT

You limit your ability to help others if you don't take care of yourself. Put on your own oxygen mask first.

©2021 Amii Barnard-Bahn

NOTES

PROMOTABILITY INDEX ELEMENT

Strategic Thinking

STRATEGIC THINKING

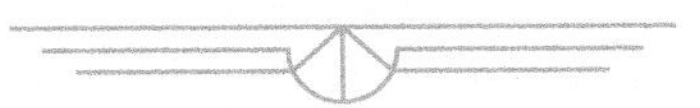

When your headlights aren't on, the best rearview mirror available isn't likely to improve your driving.

— Dr. Martha Rogers, professor and customer strategist

Strategic thinking is having a thoughtful perspective on your role and an understanding of how your organization functions, recognizing interdependencies, assessing the pros and cons of a given course of action, and tolerating ambiguity. To some degree, it also incorporates your appetite for risk taking.

Strategic thinking separates leaders from—well, from everyone else. It's a demonstrated ability to see and understand the bigger picture: where you are now, where you want to be, and how to get there. You can apply strategic thinking to both your work and your career goals to move forward.

For purposes of promotability, assessing your ability in this area involves identifying the degree to which senior management views you as a strategic thinker and asks for your input on major decisions. The benefits are significant: you gain others' trust, and leadership is comfortable giving you authority. The exercises below will help you develop your strategic thinking capability by broadening your understanding of the system you and your organization are operating in. To see around corners—to anticipate what's coming—you need to firmly understand the opportunities and constraints of your business.

You also need to assess whether you have adopted good habits in terms of applying strategic thinking to your own career. Are you staying open to a lateral move or identifying and obtaining the necessary skills for your next-level role? Some of the exercises below will help you focus on where your current career path is taking you, so that you can confirm it's headed toward your desired destination.

EXERCISES

Exercise #13: *Knowing Your Company*

What maturity stage and business cycle is your company in? ....

In one sentence, how does your company make money?

....

....

Has your company lost money over the last year? ....

The last three years? ....

With regard to achieving its current business goals, what are the top three challenges your company is facing?

....

....

....

What are key legal and ethical risks to be aware of?

....

....

INSIGHT

Create a Google alert for your company, and keep abreast of the latest news. If your company is publicly traded, read your annual shareholder report and the SEC 10K filing. These documents provide valuable information that will equip you to think and act more strategically.

Exercise #14: *Aligning with Your Boss*

What is your vision for your team?

....

....

©2021 Amii Barnard-Bahn

What is your boss's vision for your team?

....

....

How do these visions compare?

....

....

What are your boss's top three priorities for the year?

1. ....

2. ....

3. ....

How can you support your boss in achieving those priorities?

....

....

....

Exercise #15: *Supporting Company Priorities*

What current or proposed initiatives are top priorities for your management team?

....

....

How can you get involved or demonstrate your support? (For example, consider joining a cross-functional task force to address an organizational issue. If there isn't one, consider creating a task force.)

....

....

INSIGHT

You may have a fantastic idea for a project. Before rushing in to propose it, do your homework. Think a bit about the resources you'd need to execute the project, and to the extent you can, quantify the company's return on the investment. If you present your idea along with a simple cost-benefit analysis, it will lead to a much more strategic conversation.

Exercise #16: *Refreshing Your Lens*

Strategic thinking requires the ability to objectively assess your business activities and priorities from a distance. It's easy for established companies to slip into comfortable routines, product investments, and deep attachment to legacy systems. This creates resistance to change that prevents businesses from being agile, seeing around corners, and taking advantage of market disruptions and opportunity.

One great way to refresh the lens you use to view your business is to pretend that you are starting anew and have the opportunity to redesign any part of it. Use the following questions to stimulate your thinking.

What would an outsider do?

Think about the products or services you provide. Do you buy them? Why or why not?

Who are your main competitors, and what do they do differently? What can you learn from them?

INSIGHT

Use Exercise #16 as a leadership team activity to stimulate innovative thinking. It would be a useful item on the agenda of an executive retreat.

©2021 Amii Barnard-Bahn

Exercise #17: *Questioning the Status Quo*

It's exceptionally easy for companies to get stuck in their ways of doing things simply because they've always done it that way. Think about a major business process, and map out how it works.

....

....

Why does your company do it that way? ....

....

What other ways could this work get done? What could be gained by changing the process? For example: cost savings, customer satisfaction, new markets.

....

....

Exercise #18: *Thinking Ahead*

When making major decisions, such as implementing a new process or investing in a new product line, it's critical to conduct scenario planning and thoughtfully consider the impact of the proposed change on all key areas of your business, including stakeholders. Use the diagram below to map out a scenario for a new process or product. Careful planning can help reduce risk to the business, as well as improve the likelihood that your initiative is sustainable for the long term.

What new change are you designing or implementing? ....

....

What is the long-term impact of this decision on your organizational ecosphere?

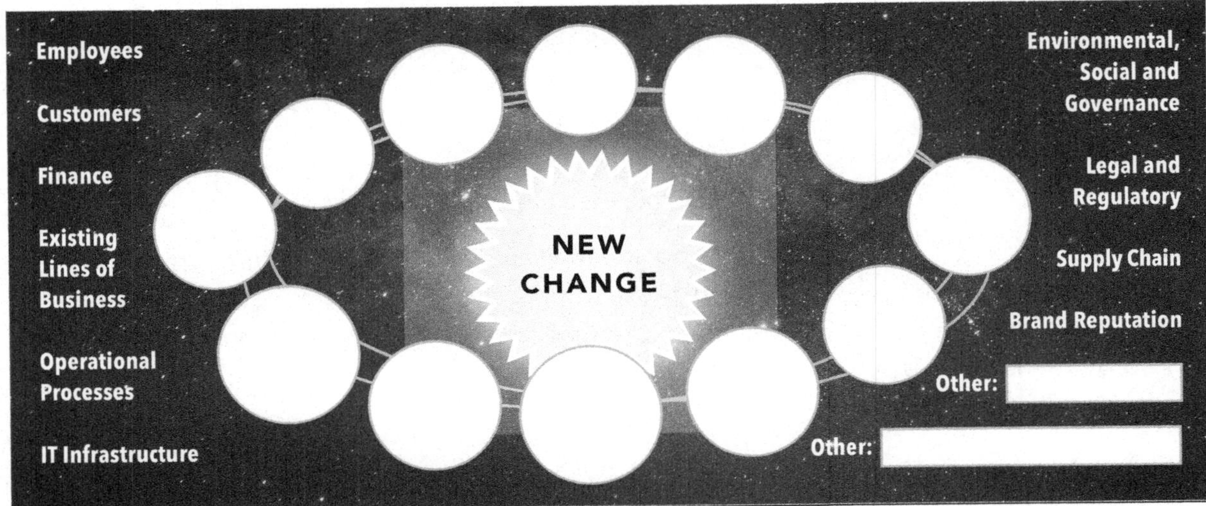

What could go wrong? Think through the worst-case scenario. Think several steps ahead with a broad picture in mind.

....

....

What tweaks can you make or what would you need to prevent or mitigate these worst-case scenarios?

....

....

Exercise #19: *Looking Back to Learn*

Think about your current job compared to the job you had a year ago. What are you doing differently?

....

....

How have your responsibilities changed?

....

....

What are three things you have learned that can take you forward in your career?

1. ....

2. ....

3. ....

INSIGHT

To really ramp up your strategic thinking capability, consider investing in a top-notch executive education program, such as those offered at Columbia Business School and Stanford Graduate School of Business. Note that many programs are online. You may also be reimbursed by your employer.

©2021 Amii Barnard-Bahn

Exercise #20: *Envisioning Your Next Step*

What type of work would you like to be doing in three years' time?

How is this different than the work you are doing now?

Talk to someone who is currently doing this work. What skills, knowledge, abilities, or network do you need to get there?

What is one step you can take now toward that goal?

INSIGHT

It can be easy to underestimate how long it takes to achieve a big goal you have set for yourself. Sometimes there are barriers we don't see. Be sure to celebrate each small win as a sign you're making progress toward your goals.

NOTES

©2021 Amii Barnard-Bahn

NOTES

PROMOTABILITY INDEX ELEMENT

Executive Presence

EXECUTIVE PRESENCE

Overcome the notion that you must be regular.
It robs you of the chance to be extraordinary.

— Uta Hagen, actress and drama teacher

This leadership element has gotten more attention as part of talent considerations over the last several years.

When you have executive presence, you establish immediate credibility with the people around you. This gives you the power to influence the level of openness people have toward your ideas and get the green light on projects. It's also the basis for cultivating respect and trust over time. That initial first impression can either accelerate a relationship or derail it.

INSIGHT

According to the Center for Talent Innovation (Coqual), executive presence can be broken down into three tangible, weighted qualities:

1. Presentation skills, or the ability to educate and engage an audience (70 percent of executive presence)
2. Gravitas, or the ability to be cool and calm under pressure (20 percent of executive presence)
3. Professional appearance, or the ability to appear well groomed and dressed appropriately for your organizational culture (10 percent of executive presence)

By incorporating these three elements, you will present yourself as an authentic, respected leader and attract other people to your network.

EXERCISES

Exercise #21: *Evaluating Your Presentation Skills*

Some people naturally thrive at public speaking, but it is mostly a skill you have to learn and practice. To be an effective presenter means connecting with your audience in a relaxed and credible way.

Of the ten items in the PI's list of presentation skills, which ones can you improve? Mark them in the checklist below.

- ☐ I maintain good eye contact when I speak with someone directly.
- ☐ When I speak, people usually stop and listen.
- ☐ I tailor my communications to the specific needs of my audience.
- ☐ I am aware of nonverbal interactions—body language like postures, gestures, and sitting positions—and what they communicate.
- ☐ I am aware of my vocal projection and make sure everyone can hear me in a room.
- ☐ I am fluent in my industry's terminology.
- ☐ I understand my organization's business goals and challenges.
- ☐ I have eliminated filler words from my vocabulary ("um," "like," "ah").
- ☐ I am aware of my vocal speech patterns and avoid those that detract from my credibility, such as poor diction, overly rapid speech, and upticks in tone at the end of a statement.
- ☐ I avoid sarcasm in speaking and writing.

Exercise #22: *Mining TED for Insights*

Search for a popular TED talk you think you'd enjoy and watch it twice—once for enjoyment and the second time for taking notes. Then answer the following questions:

What do you notice about the speaker's physical presence? How do they stand? How do they use the stage? Do they maintain eye contact with the audience?

....

....

What do you notice about the speaker's voice inflection—volume, cadence, diction, and the power of the pause. How do they use their voice as a tool for emphasis and to create an emotional hook with the audience?

....

....

©2021 Amii Barnard-Bahn

If they use slides, how did their use of this visual imagery enhance your engagement with their topic?

....

What else did you notice that made this speaker particularly effective? Did you notice anything that detracted from their impact?

....

....

INSIGHT

My favorite TED talk is Nancy Duarte's *The Secret Structure of Great Talks* (ted.com/talks/nancy_duarte_the_secret_structure_of_great_talks). It forever changed the way I deliver presentations and keynotes.

Exercise #23: *Rehearsing Your Presentation*

Before your next big presentation, practice it in front of a camera. If you don't have an upcoming talk, spend two minutes recording yourself describing what your company does. Record yourself using your mobile phone, laptop, or other device. Then watch the replay three times.

The *first time*, watch yourself with the sound off, and write down your observations. Focus on your body language, such as eye contact and physical stance, and evaluate it for how well it communicates ease and confidence. Watch for any distracting physical tics, such as swaying side-to-side, head nodding, or foot tapping.

....

....

The *second time*, listen with the video off, and write down your observations. Focus just on your voice. Are you using it to maximum effect? How is your enunciation?

....

....

Should any words be changed for greater audience comprehension or impact? Keep a close watch for verbal filler words such as "um," "uh," and "like."

....

....

The third time, watch the video with the sound on, and make any final notes, using the prompts in *Exercise 21* (page 46).

....

....

INSIGHT

If your presentation will be in person, try to re-create the actual room setup. Make sustained eye contact with one specific person in each area of the room for about three to five seconds. If you are presenting virtually, technology can actually make eye-contact magic: look directly at the camera, and you are looking at everyone at the same time.

When presenting on video, I hide my self-view so I can focus on connecting with my audience. If I'm presenting slides, I also move the minimized audience view and place it right under my computer camera so I am making solid eye contact by looking right into the camera. Some people tape a photo of their kids or pets near the camera lens to help them smile and relax and to focus their eyes in the right place.

Preparation and practice are the best way to ensure a successful outcome and to get over any presentation jitters you may have. The more you practice, the more natural and warm you will seem in front of a group. Rehearse until it's natural and becomes more of a conversation.

Exercise #24: *Enlisting a Constructive Critic*

Ask a trusted colleague, a family member, someone from your company's PR team, or your coach to watch you present and give you feedback on your body language, volume, audience engagement, and other critical factors for successful presentations.

Effective presenting is all about being comfortable with your subject matter—and sharing it in a way that inspires your audience to care about what you have to say. If your reviewer is remote, send them a copy of your recording for their feedback. If you have a specific behavior you're working to improve, ask them to focus on that.

Ask your reviewer to use the checklist and questions below to evaluate your presentation.

- ☐ Good posture
- ☐ Confident physical stance
- ☐ High energy
- ☐ Warm presence that connects with the audience
- ☐ Effective vocal projection
- ☐ Good enunciation
- ☐ Varied vocal inflection
- ☐ Appropriate hand gestures
- ☐ Good eye contact
- ☐ Avoided empty filler words ("um," "like," "ah")

©2021 Amii Barnard-Bahn

Any detracting behaviors? ....

....

Did the presentation keep your attention? ....

....

Any areas where delivery or content lagged and needs juice? ....

....

Exercise #25: *Gaining Experience*

If you don't currently present regularly to an audience, now is the time to get out there! Professional organizations are always seeking great content, and it's a low-risk way to improve your public speaking and build your network at the same time. First, you'll want to identify speaking topics that are a good match for your professional expertise, and then you can look for opportunities to use your expertise. For starters, look at professional associations, alumni groups, and options inside your company, such as employee resource groups.

Complete the sentences on the next page to set your personal goals for gaining experience in presenting.

I am an expert in ....

I would be interested in speaking on ....

Groups that might be interested in my expertise are...

....

....

....

I will reach out to the following organizations ....

I will do so by .... date.

If there are several groups you want to connect with, you may want to set a monthly target.

INSIGHT

To be an engaging and dynamic presenter, you will want to connect with your audience in a personal and engaging way. Repetition and practice are key. You should know the message so well that you can forget about the content and focus on creating a personal connection.

Exercise #26: *Identifying Triggers*

Because people are attracted to leaders who remain cool and calm under pressure, allowing emotional triggers to negatively impact your leadership presence can hurt you in a professional setting.

Start noticing what sets you off. In coaching terms, we call this an "emotional hook." We all have hooks, based on our upbringing, history, and personality, that can irritate us or, worse, cause us to blow up or shut down. If we don't learn how to manage our triggers, they will impact how we show up as leaders.

Think about the last time you lost your temper at work. Perhaps you judged a team member harshly for making a bad choice, or you felt envious of a work colleague's success. Pick one emotional reaction that is not serving you, and start noticing when this behavior is triggered. Keep a journal for a week and identify one behavior trigger. Note the circumstances of the event and thoughts that came to mind. Chances are, your internal emotions are showing up externally. Recognizing the pattern is the first step to choosing an alternative reaction. (Use the *Awareness Journal* on the next page.)

©2021 Amii Barnard-Bahn

AWARENESS JOURNAL

Context: Give a brief description of the situation surrounding the event that didn't go as you'd hoped—include who, what, where, and when.

Beliefs: What did you tell yourself or feel at the time?

Reactions: What did you do or say at the time?

Reflect: What is the impact of your reaction? Are your beliefs, thoughts, and reactions manifesting the outcome you want?

Action: Based on what you've observed, what choice do you want to make next time?

Exercise #27: *Dressing with Power*

I'm a big believer in dressing for the role you want, not the one you currently have. Whether we like it or not, behavioral science research repeatedly shows that for a person to be accepted as part of a group, the group has to feel comfortable with them. How you dress can affect a group's comfort level with you.

Context is important. If you're working for a startup in Silicon Valley, your CEO may wear T-shirts and expensive jeans with flip flops. If you're on Wall Street, we may be talking bespoke suits. Know your audience, and be conscious of the dress code. Too many people think the clothes you wear don't matter. That's generally only true after you've made it to where you want to be.

What do you notice about how senior management dresses at your organization?

....

....

Are there any tweaks or changes you'd like to make to your work wardrobe or personal styling?

....

....

INSIGHT

Culture, identity, religion, personal finances, and our upbringing play a huge role in how we dress and groom ourselves. Women, people of color, expatriates working in a foreign culture, people with disabilities, and many others face an extra burden when trying to fit in to the workplace. Be true to yourself, and find the culture fit that is right for you.

Exercise #28: *Identifying Role Models*

Who are three people that you admire that currently have the role (or a similar one) you aspire to?

1. ....
2. ....
3. ....

©2021 Amii Barnard-Bahn

Go online and find their social media profiles. What do you notice about their appearance in professional photos?

....

....

....

How are they groomed? If you have the opportunity to be around them, notice how they are groomed for important business meetings. Write down your observations.

....

....

Exercise #29: *Getting a Good Headshot*

How good is your professional headshot? Evaluate it based on the following criteria:

- ☐ Good lighting, full on face (no strong, dramatic shadows or fuzzy images).
- ☐ You are looking directly into the camera. Virtual eye contact!
- ☐ The background is neutral; the focus is on you. Remember you are building trust and making a first impression.
- ☐ The image frames your head just below your shoulders.

INSIGHT

To make your headshots pop, pick a shirt or jacket color that contrasts against your skin tone, instead of one that blends in. Solids are a safe bet; avoid busy patterns or heavy jewelry that distracts from your face and that can look dated quickly.

Don't let your photographer photoshop out wrinkles, heavily airbrush, or use dramatic studio lighting.

If it's been more than eighteen months since your last headshot, consider getting a new one.

Make sure you update your photo internally at your organization and across all social media, board member directories, and professional association networks.

NOTES

©2021 Amii Barnard-Bahn

NOTES

PROMOTABILITY INDEX ELEMENT

Thought Leadership

THOUGHT LEADERSHIP

The things you do for yourself are gone when you are gone.
But the things you do for others remain as your legacy.

— Kalu Ndukwe Kalu, political scientist

It's rewarding, both professionally and personally, to be known as an expert. Thought leadership establishes your identity as a contributor, someone who is forward-thinking and influential in your domain expertise. Thought leadership also leads to tangible rewards. Your professional currency rises with your evolution as a thought leader because your skills are proven to be marketable, your network is strong, and speaking and other professional engagement opportunities, such as corporate board service, come more easily.

EXERCISES

Exercise #30: *Identifying Your Superpower*

What is your superpower? Think about what you are known for, or what problems people come to you to solve, either at work or in your personal life.

....

....

Exercise #31: *Sharing Your Expertise*

How do you currently share your thoughts and expertise?

....

....

What is a respected audience you'd like to speak for or a publication you'd love to write for?

....

What is an area you'd like to write or speak about?

....

Identify an opportunity, and commit to a timeline:

....

Exercise #32: *Connecting with Thought Leaders*

Name three leaders you admire in your industry or profession:

1. ....
2. ....
3. ....

Are you connected to them? If not, how can you become a welcomed part of their network? For example, you can share their ideas, write about them in a social media post, or interview them for an article.

....

....

....

©2021 Amii Barnard-Bahn

Exercise #33: *Developing Leadership Skills Through Meaningful Service*

What is a charitable cause that is meaningful to you?

....

Identify three organizations that serve your meaningful purpose.

1. ....
2. ....
3. ....

What is one step you could take toward helping them?

....

INSIGHT

My earliest leadership roles started with nonprofit boards. In addition to being deeply rewarding, serving on a board is a valuable training ground where you can develop key organizational skills that will help your career.

NOTES

©2021 Amii Barnard-Bahn

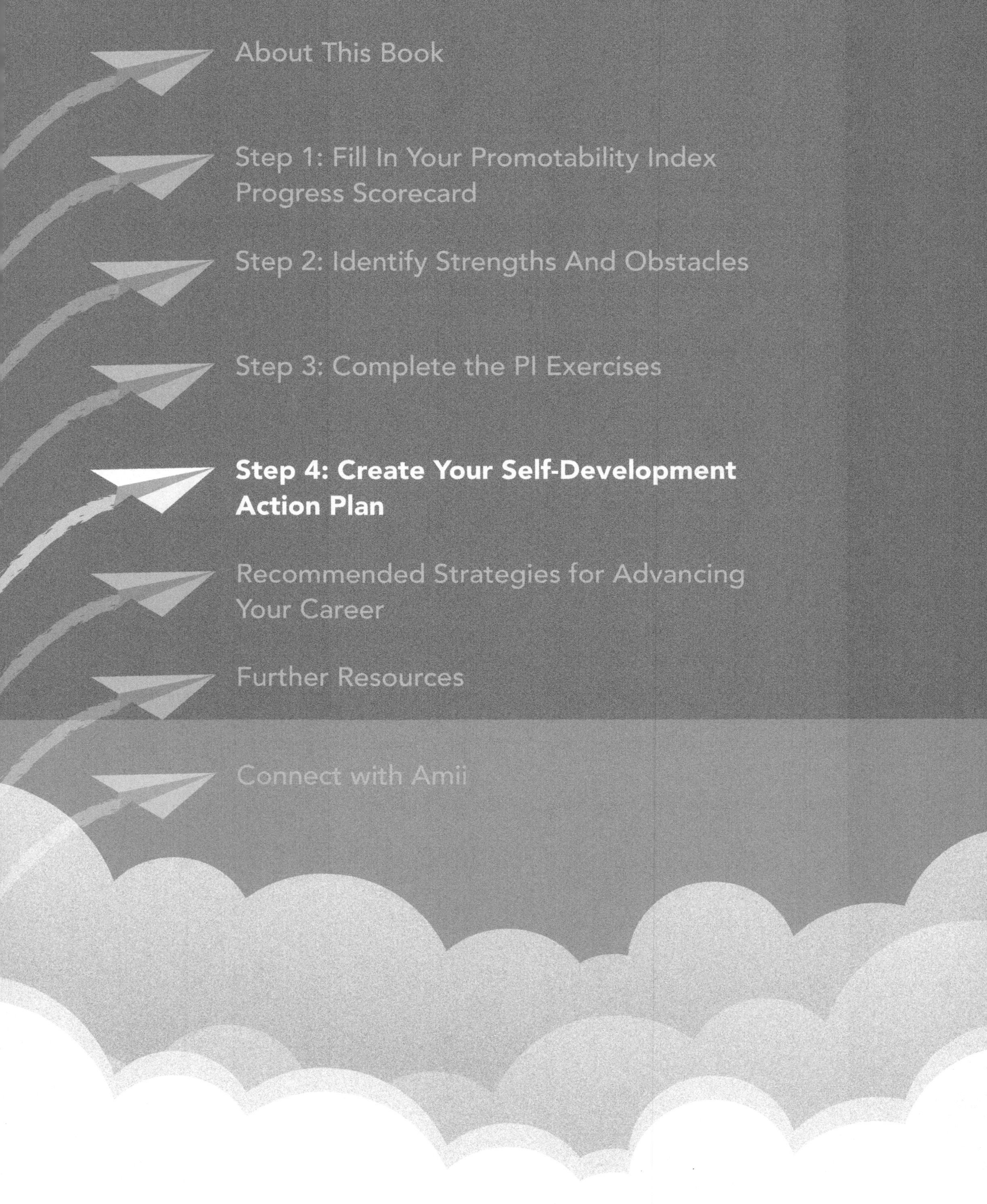
About This Book
Step 1: Fill In Your Promotability Index Progress Scorecard
Step 2: Identify Strengths And Obstacles
Step 3: Complete the PI Exercises
Step 4: Create Your Self-Development Action Plan
Recommended Strategies for Advancing Your Career
Further Resources
Connect with Amii

STEP 4

CREATE YOUR SELF-DEVELOPMENT ACTION PLAN

This is where you commit to taking action!

Be sure to choose only one or two elements to work on. You want to focus on small shifts that add up over time. Incremental changes lead to a deeper transformation.

Consider incorporating your action plan into your company's performance review process for extra support and to help you align your professional goals with your employer's plans.

Post your goal and action plan where you can see it every day.

Break your annual plan into quarterly goals that are SMART:

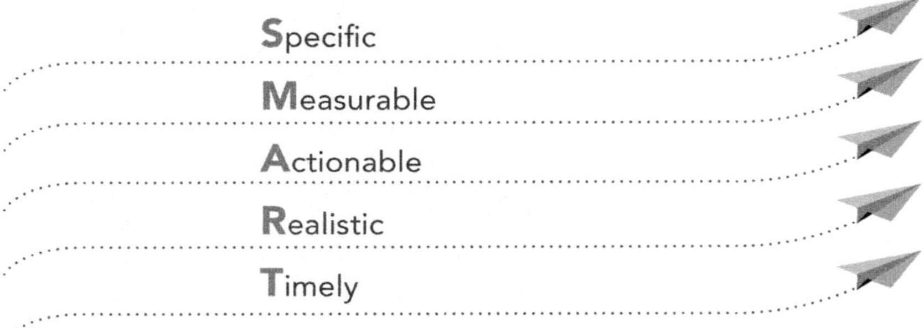

Block time on your calendar toward the end of every quarter to spend at least one hour reviewing your goals. Record actions you took in furtherance of your goal.

Be sure to update your annual plan based on your progress toward your goals. You may find something that needs to shift or change; that's normal. Sometimes an opportunity may present itself that takes priority over a goal you had in mind. Stay flexible and focused. Revise your plan, and review the results.

Hold yourself accountable for the big things. Let the small stuff go.

©2021 Amii Barnard-Bahn

ACTION PLAN

Date: ....

My goal for the next .... weeks is to improve in the following key elements (choose up to two out of the five):

☐ Self-Awareness	☐ External Awareness	☐ Strategic Thinking
☐ Executive Presence	☐ Thought Leadership	
Notes on steps to take:		

I will commit to completing the following exercises by the following dates:

Key Element .... Exercise # .... by ....

Key Element .... Exercise # .... by ....

Key Element .... Exercise # .... by ....

Key Element .... Exercise # .... by ....

To improve, I will take the following actions:

....

....

....

Potential obstacles (from page 13):

....

....

....

Strengths I can leverage to overcome these obstacles (from page 12):

....

....

....

Give yourself a deadline. Pick a target date that challenges you a bit but is realistic.

I will do this by ....

How will you know you've achieved your goal? What is a tangible outcome?

I will know I'm successful when ....

©2021 Amii Barnard-Bahn

NOTES

NOTES

©2021 Amii Barnard-Bahn

RECOMMENDED STRATEGIES FOR ADVANCING YOUR CAREER

Timing is everything. While you can work on your skills any time, asking your boss about what's next for your career usually requires some finesse.

Have an honest and open career discussion with your boss regarding next steps. Pick your timing well (not when they are preparing for a challenging board meeting), and schedule it in advance. For example, when I was working for a corporation, I would check in midyear and ask to talk about my career development. I wanted to learn what I didn't know and what I didn't see.

Having this conversation outside of my annual personnel review took the pressure off pay and promotions, making the conversation truly developmental (rather than evaluative) and enabling candor. I did this every year, so my bosses came to expect it, and it helped me continue to learn, be challenged, and successively get promoted over time.

If you've been in your role for three to five years and your growth or access to challenging work is declining, it may be time to consider a change. Lateral moves (without a pay raise) are often required to pick up key skills that later help you rise up and significantly spike progress in your career. Sometimes even taking a temporary step backward to pick up an important skill may be required for long-term advancement. Before advancing to the C-suite, I did both—I made a lateral move, and I took a lower position temporarily.

If advancement is not possible at your company—you've gotten as far as you can or your company is experiencing a downturn in its business—you may need to decide whether to hold in place or make an external leap.

Sometimes it makes sense to stay. You may be getting the experience you need at this time in your career, or perhaps you love your organization and are biding your time to see if a promotion is in the cards. Consciously waiting it out is a respectable strategy. Just set a timeline that feels comfortable to you, and keep learning during this time.

Being promotable is all about being responsible for your impact. Use the exercises in this book, revisit the ones that work for you, and move toward what calls to you. Hold yourself accountable, and keep taking actions to move forward. If you do, you are pretty much guaranteed to get results.

Summon the courage, and do the work. Surround yourself with people who believe in you. Be kind to yourself, and be kind to others.

And while you can make significant progress on your own, particularly as you move into executive roles and the C-suite, some leadership behaviors and skills often become hard to improve without help. At a certain point, we all get stuck in a pattern that is not serving us, we aren't getting the feedback we need to grow, or we lose momentum. This is when engaging an executive coach is a wise investment in yourself and for those around you. I know because this is exactly what I did. The results were exponential—personally and professionally—and led me to becoming a professional coach.

For more insights, visit *barnardbahn.com.*

©2021 Amii Barnard-Bahn

NOTES

NOTES

©2021 Amii Barnard-Bahn

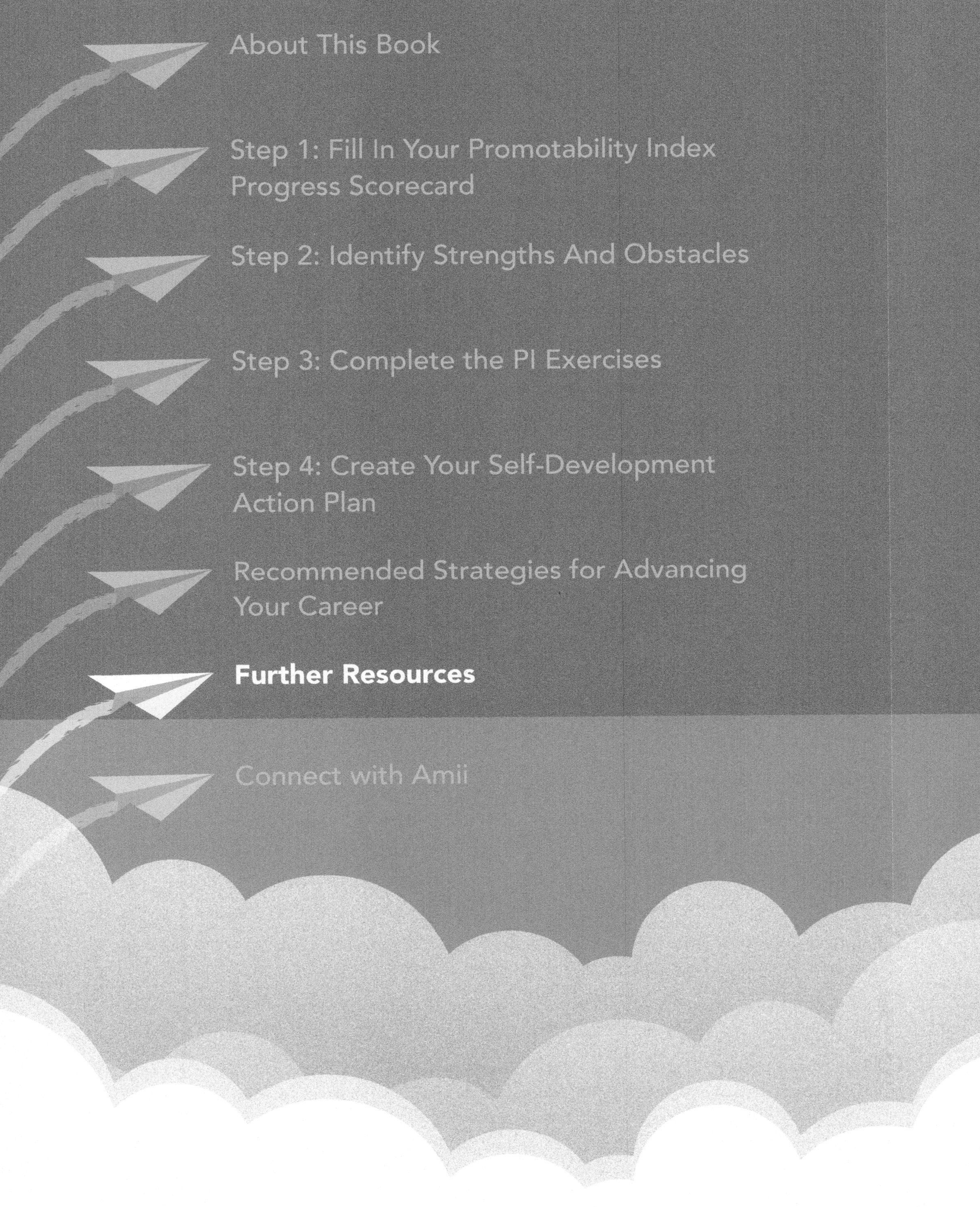
About This Book
Step 1: Fill In Your Promotability Index Progress Scorecard
Step 2: Identify Strengths And Obstacles
Step 3: Complete the PI Exercises
Step 4: Create Your Self-Development Action Plan
Recommended Strategies for Advancing Your Career
Further Resources
Connect with Amii

FURTHER RESOURCES

These are my top recommended resources, listed by PI subject area and in order of recommended reading. For example, fundamental resources are listed first, and then more complex or specialized readings—such as resources specifically for women—are listed later.

IDENTIFYING AND LEVERAGING STRENGTHS

- Tom Rath. *StrengthsFinder 2.0*. New York: Gallup, 2007.
- Carol S. Dweck. *Mindset: The New Psychology of Success*. New York: Ballantine, 2016.
- Jim Loehr. *The Power of Story: Change Your Story, Change Your Destiny in Business and Life*. New York: Free Press, 2007.
- Robert J. Anderson and William A. Adams. *Mastering Leadership: An Integrated Framework for Breakthrough Performance and Extraordinary Business Results*. Hoboken, NJ: John Wiley & Sons, 2016.
- Herminia Ibarra. *Working Identity: Unconventional Strategies for Reinventing Your Career*. Boston: Harvard Business School Press, 2003.
- Jeffrey Hull. *Flex: The Art and Science of Leadership in a Changing World*. New York: TarcherPerigee, 2019.
- Frederic M. Hudson. *The Adult Years: Mastering the Art of Self-Renewal*. Revised edition. San Francisco: Jossey-Bass, 1999.

OVERCOMING OBSTACLES

- Robert Kegan and Lisa Lahey. "The Real Reason People Won't Change." *Harvard Business Review*. November 2001. hbr.org/2001/11/the-real-reason-people-wont-change.
- David L. Dotlich and Peter C. Cairo. *Why CEOs Fail: The 11 Behaviors That Can Derail Your Climb to the Top—and How to Manage Them*. San Francisco: Jossey-Bass, 2003.
- Whitney Johnson. *Disrupt Yourself: Master Relentless Change and Speed Up Your Learning Curve*. Boston: Harvard Business School Press, 2020.
- Kerry Patterson, Joseph Grenny, Ron McMillan, and Al Switzler. *Crucial Conversations: Tools for Talking When Stakes Are High*. New York: McGraw Hill, 2012.
- Carla Harris. *How to Find the Person Who Can Help You Get Ahead at Work*. Talk presented at TEDWomen, November 2018. TED video, 13:15. ted.com/talks/carla_harris_how_to_find_the_person_who_can_help_you_get_ahead_at_work.

©2021 Amii Barnard-Bahn

- Max H. Bazerman and Ann E. Tenbrunsel. *Blind Spots: Why We Fail to Do What's Right and What to Do About It*. Princeton, NJ: Princeton University Press, 2011.
- Bryan E. Robinson. *Chained to the Desk: A Guidebook for Workaholics, Their Partners and Children, and the Clinicians Who Treat Them*. 3rd edition. New York: New York University Press, 2014.

SELF-AWARENESS

- Daniel Goleman. *Emotional Intelligence: Why It Can Matter More Than IQ*. 10th anniversary edition. New York: Bantam, 2006.
- Marshall Goldsmith. *What Got You Here Won't Get You There*. New York: Hyperion, 2007.
- Sally Helgesen and Marshall Goldsmith. *How Women Rise: Break the 12 Habits Holding You Back from Your Next Raise, Promotion, or Job*. New York: Hachette, 2018.
- Tasha Eurich. *Insight: The Surprising Truth About How Others See Us, How We See Ourselves, and Why the Answers Matter More Than We Think*. New York: Currency, 2018.
- Susan David. *Emotional Agility: Get Unstuck, Embrace Change, and Thrive in Work and Life*. New York: Avery, 2016.
- *HBR's 10 Must Reads: On Managing Yourself*. Boston: Harvard Business School Publishing, 2010.

EXTERNAL AWARENESS

- Marilee Adams. *Change Your Questions, Change Your Life: 12 Powerful Tools for Leadership, Coaching, and Life*. 3rd edition. Oakland, CA: Berrett-Koehler, 2015.
- Douglas Stone and Sheila Heen. *Thanks for the Feedback: The Science and Art of Receiving Feedback Well*. New York: Penguin, 2014.
- Michael J. Gelb. *The Art of Connection: 7 Relationship-Building Skills Every Leader Needs Now*. Novato, CA: New World Library, 2017.
- Keith Ferrazzi. *Never Eat Alone, and Other Secrets to Success, One Relationship at a Time*. New York: Currency, 2014.
- Alison Wood Brooks and Leslie K. John. "The Surprising Power of Questions." *Harvard Business Review*. May–June 2018. hbr.org/2018/05/the-surprising-power-of-questions.

STRATEGIC THINKING

- Rita McGrath. *Seeing Around Corners: How to Spot Inflection Points in Business Before They Happen*. New York: Houghton Mifflin Harcourt, 2019.
- *HBR's 10 Must Reads: On Strategy*. Vol. 2. Boston: Harvard Business School Publishing, 2020.

Jennifer Garvey Berger and Keith Johnston. *Simple Habits for Complex Times: Powerful Practices for Leaders*. Stanford, CA: Stanford University Press, 2015.

Oleg Konovalov. *The Vision Code: How to Create and Execute a Compelling Vision for Your Business*. Chicester, UK: John Wiley & Sons, 2021.

Peter Sims. *Little Bets: How Breakthrough Ideas Emerge from Small Discoveries*. New York: Simon & Schuster, 2011.

Bill Burnett and Dave Evans. *Designing Your Life: How to Build a Well-Lived, Joyful Life*. New York: Borzoi Books, 2016.

EXECUTIVE PRESENCE

Michael J. Gelb. *Mastering the Art of Public Speaking: 8 Secrets to Transform Fear and Supercharge Your Career*. Novato, CA: New World Library, 2020.

Katty Kay and Claire Shipman. *The Confidence Code: The Science and Art of Self-Assurance—What Women Should Know*. New York: HarperCollins, 2014.

Marshall Goldsmith and Mark Reiter. *Triggers: Creating Behavior That Lasts—Becoming the Person You Want to Be*. New York: Crown Business, 2015.

Marilyn Gist. *The Extraordinary Power of Leader Humility*. Oakland, CA: Berrett-Koehler, 2020.

Carla Harris. *The Power of Authenticity*. Produced by APB Speakers, August 13, 2019. YouTube video, 3:24. youtube.com/watch?v=OEnEOOgXA2M.

THOUGHT LEADERSHIP

Dorie Clark. *Reinventing You: Define Your Brand, Imagine Your Future*. Boston: Harvard Business School Publishing, 2013.

Robert B. Cialdini. *Influence: The Psychology of Persuasion*. Revised edition. New York: Harper Business, 2006.

Denise Brosseau. *Ready to Be a Thought Leader? How to Increase Your Influence, Impact, and Success*. San Francisco: Jossey-Bass, 2013.

Frances Hesselbein, Marshall Goldsmith, and Iain Somerville (editors). *Leading Beyond the Walls*. San Francisco: Jossey-Bass, 1999.

Nancy Duarte. *The Secret Structure of Great Talks*. Talk presented at TEDxEast, November 2011. TED video, 18:01. ted.com/talks/nancy_duarte_the_secret_structure_of_great_talks.

©2021 Amii Barnard-Bahn

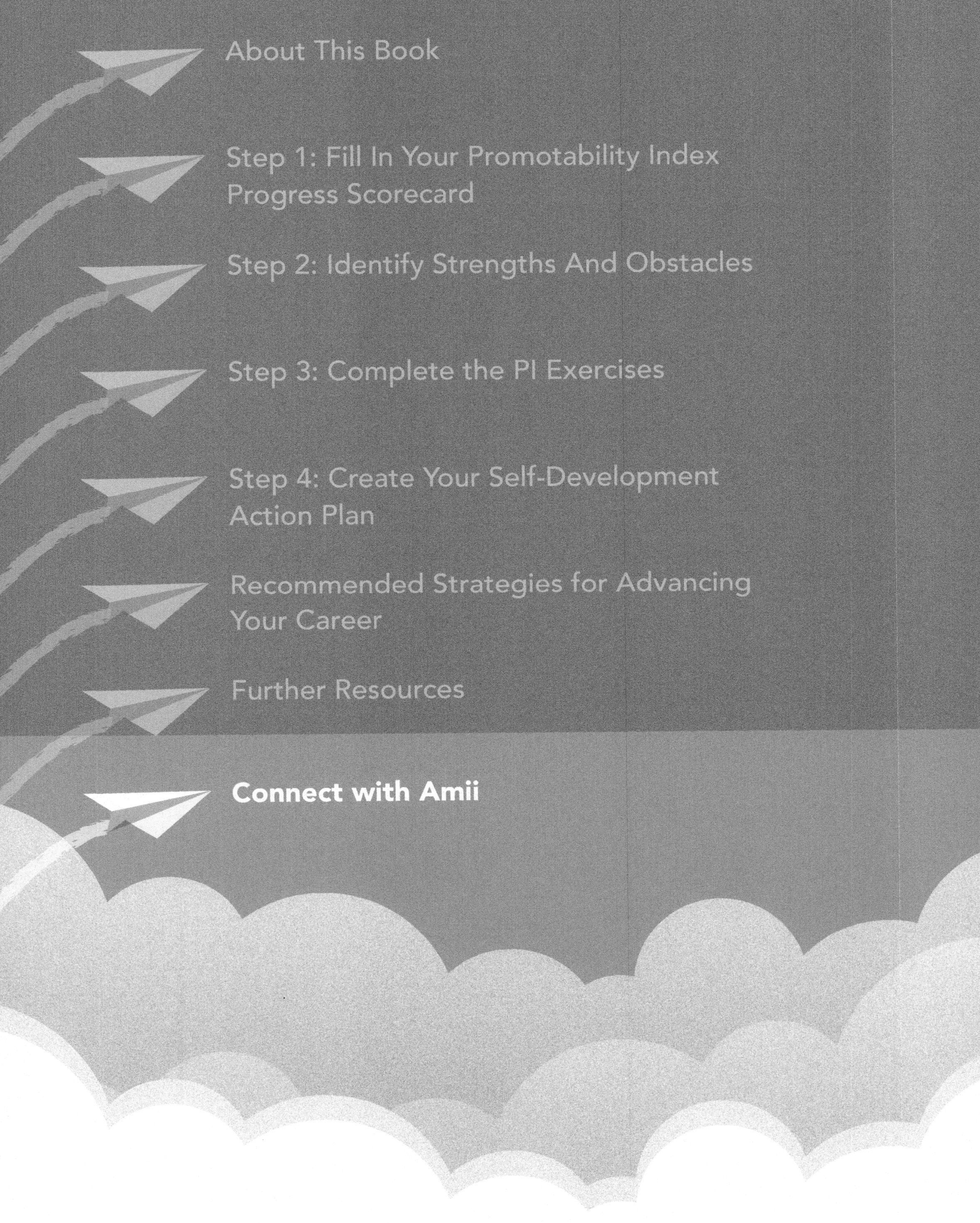
About This Book
Step 1: Fill In Your Promotability Index Progress Scorecard
Step 2: Identify Strengths And Obstacles
Step 3: Complete the PI Exercises
Step 4: Create Your Self-Development Action Plan
Recommended Strategies for Advancing Your Career
Further Resources
Connect with Amii

CONNECT WITH AMII

I want to hear about your progress and what's working for you. There are many ways to stay connected with me.

Visit the Promotability Index website (*barnardbahn.com/promotabilityindex*).

Sign up for my newsletter (*bit.ly/newsfromamii*).

Check out my Resources page (*barnardbahn.com/resources*), where I post articles, podcasts, videos, and other resources.

Connect with me on social media:

- amiibarnardbahn (*linkedin.com/in/amiibarnardbahn*)
- @amiibb (*twitter.com/amiibb*)
- @barnardbahn (*instagram.com/barnardbahn*)
- Subscribe to my YouTube channel (*bit.ly/amiibarnardbahn*).

When you're on social media, I'd encourage you to use the hashtag *#PromotabilityIndex* to connect with me as well as others using the PI.

©2021 Amii Barnard-Bahn

NOTES

NOTES

©2021 Amii Barnard-Bahn

NOTES

NOTES

©2021 Amii Barnard-Bahn

NOTES

NOTES

©2021 Amii Barnard-Bahn

NOTES

ABOUT THE AUTHOR

AMII BARNARD-BAHN is an executive coach and consultant who specializes in accelerating the success of Fortune 500 executives and their teams at clients such as Adobe, Bank of the West, and The Gap. A recognized expert in workplace culture, corporate governance, and ethical leadership, she partners with leaders, teams, and boards in the US and abroad to successfully shape and support business strategy and performance excellence.

She received her JD from Georgetown and has been recognized by *Forbes* as one of the top coaches for legal and compliance executives. Amii is a contributor to *Harvard Business Review*, *Fast Company*, and *Compliance Week*. She guest lectures at Stanford and UC Berkeley and is a Fellow at the Institute of Coaching, McLean/Harvard Medical School.

Amii is a member of Marshall Goldsmith's 100 Coaches, an invitation-only community that brings together the world's top executive coaches and whose mission is to inspire, develop, and energize leaders for the future.

For twenty years Amii shaped company culture and strategy as an executive in multiple roles at Fortune 50 global companies. A lifelong diversity advocate, Amii testified in multiple committees on the successful passage of the first US laws requiring corporate boards to include women.

She lives with her husband and two daughters in Sacramento, California.

©2021 Amii Barnard-Bahn

Made in the USA
Coppell, TX
28 May 2021

56314828R00052